IT'S ELECTRIC!

ELECTRIC BOATS

Scott Wilken

Big Buddy Books
An Imprint of Abdo Publishing
abdobooks.com

abdobooks.com

Published by Abdo Publishing, a division of ABDO, PO Box 398166, Minneapolis, Minnesota 55439.

Printed in the United States of America, North Mankato, Minnesota
052023
092023

THIS BOOK CONTAINS RECYCLED MATERIALS

Design: Sarah DeYoung, Mighty Media, Inc.
Production: Mighty Media, Inc.
Editor: Katherine Chu
Cover Photograph: Igor Karasi/Shutterstock Images
Interior Photographs: Albert Tissandier/Wikimedia Commons, pp. 5, 28 (Electric boat by Gustave Trouvé); allanw/Shutterstock Images, pp. 13, 28 (Duffy); Dr. Karl-Heinz Hochhaus/Wikimedia Commons, p. 27; Ian Dewar Photography/Shutterstock Images, p. 11; Magnus Johansson/Flickr, pp. 18–19; Zenpenofoto/Shutterstock Images, p. 17; Philip Pilosian/Shutterstock Images, p. 9; Phuketian.S/Shutterstock Images, pp. 23, 25; Saint-ex/Wikimedia Commons, p. 21; Trygve Finkelsen/Shutterstock Images, p. 15; Yalcin Sonat/Shutterstock Images, p. 7
Design Elements: octopusaga/Shutterstock Images (hexagon pattern); Vlad Malinovskij/Shutterstock Images (lightning bolt icon); Zoa.Arts/Shutterstock Images (lightning)

Library of Congress Control Number: 2022948825

Publisher's Cataloging-in-Publication Data
Names: Wilken, Scott, author.
Title: Electric boats / by Scott Wilken
Description: Minneapolis, Minnesota : Abdo Publishing, 2024 | Series: It's electric! | Includes online resources and index.
Identifiers: ISBN 9781098291525 (lib. bdg.) | ISBN 9781098277987 (ebook)
Subjects: LCSH: Electric boats--Juvenile literature. | Boats--Juvenile literature. | Electric vehicles--Juvenile literature. | Boats and boating--Juvenile literature. | Transportation--Juvenile literature.
Classification: DDC 388--dc23

CONTENTS

CHAPTER 1

SMOOTH & SILENT

Your friend invited you on a boat ride. You take a seat, wondering when the boat will leave. When you look over, the shore is far away! But you don't hear a sound or feel any movement. That's because the boat is an electric **vehicle** (EV)!

FAST FACT

The first electric boats were invented in the 1800s. They were popular until more powerful gas-powered boats were built in the late 1800s.

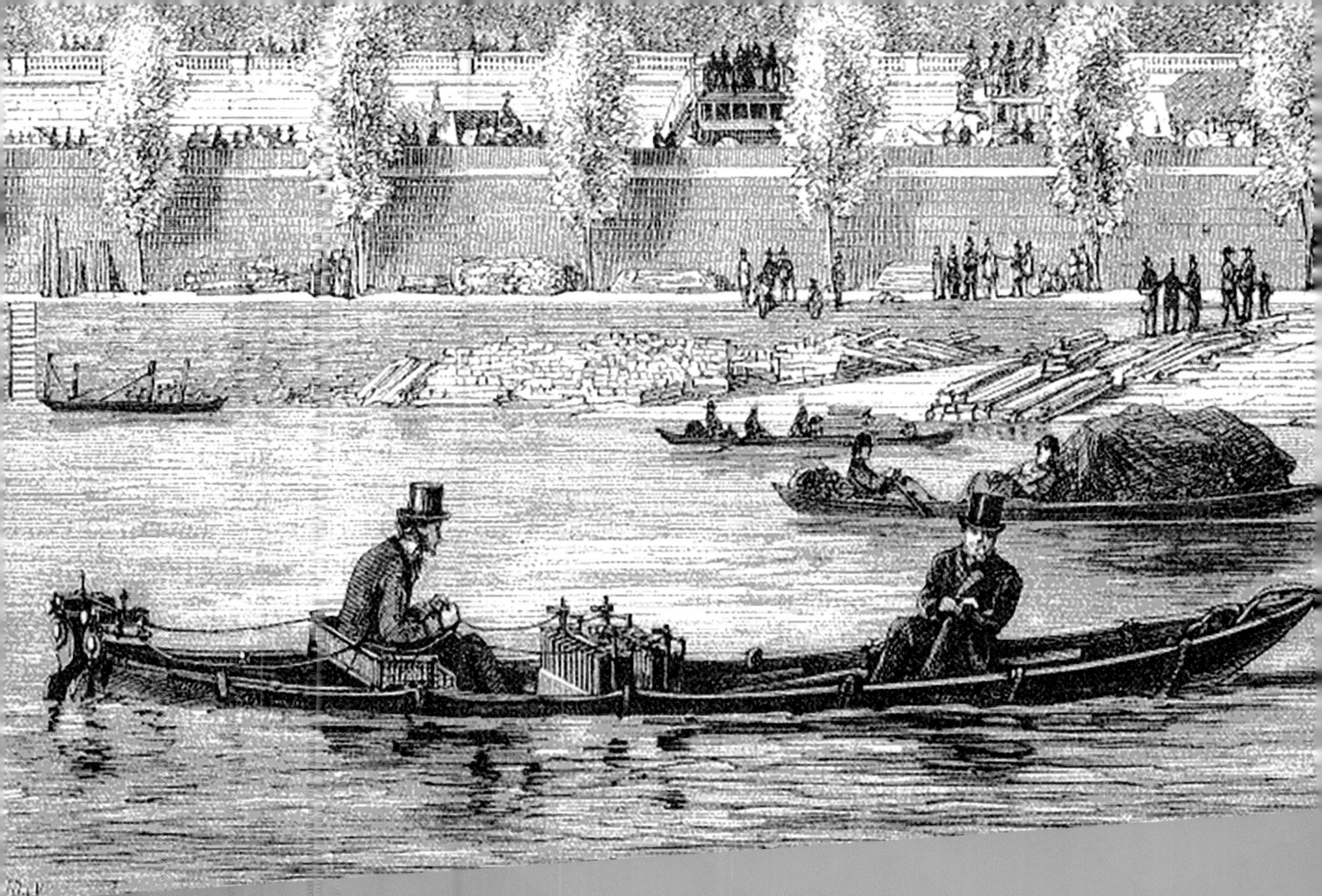

French inventor Gustave Trouvé was one of the first people to build an electric boat.

CHAPTER 2

WHY ELECTRIC?

An EV's **motor** is powered by electricity. The electricity is stored in **rechargeable batteries**. In recent years, electric boats have become popular for a few reasons.

Gas **vehicles release** gases that harm Earth. EVs do not. And charging an EV costs less than buying gas. Modern electric boats have also become more advanced than earlier models.

Many marinas have charging stations to charge onboard electronics. Some stations can be used to charge electric boats.

CHAPTER 3

DUFFY LEADS THE WAY

Some of the first modern electric boats were made by Duffy Electric Boats in 1970. The California-based company called its boats "Duffys." The boats were powered by 6-**volt batteries**. They also had built-in battery chargers.

FAST FACT

An electric boat uses more power the faster it goes. It can go longer between charges at slower speeds.

Marshall "Duffy" Duffield's first electric boat was powered by a motor from a golf cart.

In 2022, Duffy offered five different models. The lengths of the models ranged from 16.5 feet to 22 feet (5 to 6.7 m). A Duffy boat's top speed is about 5 to 6 miles per hour (8 to 9.7 kmh). Depending on the model, it can be driven for 3.5 to 12.5 hours before the **batteries** need to be charged.

Since 1970, Duffy has made more than 10,000 electric boats.

Duffy boats travel best on calm water. They are ideal for lakes, rivers, and bays. Depending on the model, Duffy boats can carry 8 to 12 adults.

Duffy boats are also built to be comfortable and last a long time. Duffy buyers can enjoy taking boat trips with friends and family.

Duffy makes boats for many different venues. They include Disney's California Adventure Park and many Marriott hotels.

CHAPTER 4

SPEEDY SAILING

In the 1990s, scientists **developed lithium-ion batteries** that could power **vehicles**. In the 2010s, boat companies started making boat **motors** using these batteries. Swedish company X Shore made two models. These are the Eelex 8000 and the X Shore 1.

FAST FACT

Lithium-ion batteries are powerful. They allow boats to go faster and travel farther.

In 2018, X Shore launched its first boat model. The model later became the Eelex 8000.

The Eelex 8000 was **released** in 2020. It is about 26 feet (8 m) long. The X Shore 1 was released in 2022. It is 21 feet (6.5 m) long. Both models can be used on the ocean as well as on lakes and rivers. They need to **recharge** their **batteries** using onshore charging stations.

X Shore took inspiration from South American electric eels when creating the Eelex 8000.

EELEX 8000

Starting price: $329,000

Top speed: 35 miles per hour (56.3 kmh)

Range: Up to 115.1 miles (185.2 km) on one charge

Motor: 170 kilowatts

Charging time: About one to eight hours to charge from 20% to 80%, depending on charger

Statistics from 2022 model

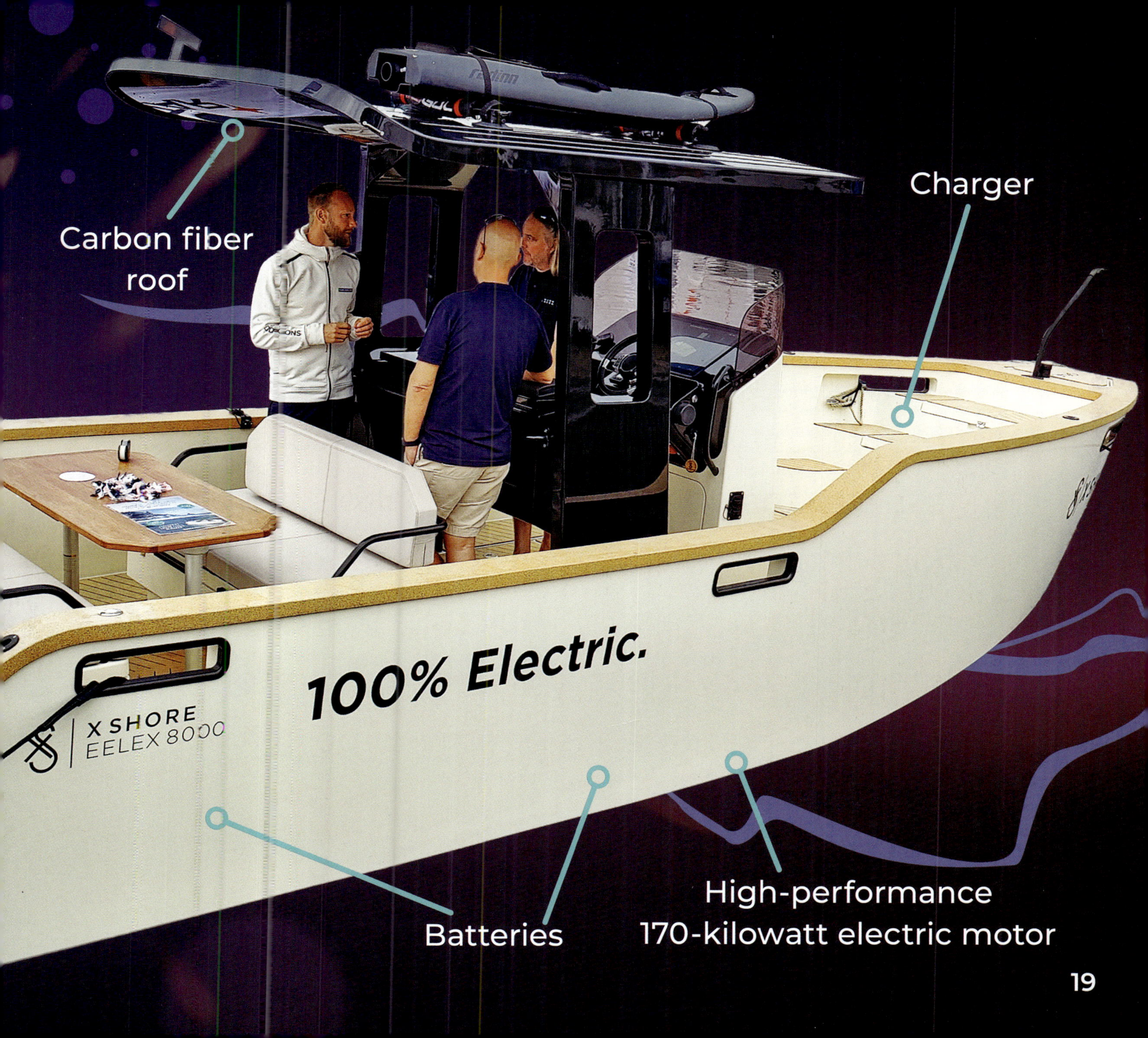

Carbon fiber roof
Charger
100% Electric.
X SHORE
EELEX 8000
Batteries
High-performance 170-kilowatt electric motor

CHAPTER 5

SUN POWER

The first solar-powered boat was created in 1975. This type of boat grew in popularity when solar panels became less **expensive** in 2010. Solar panels are flat surfaces with special cells that collect energy from the sun. They turn this energy into electricity. Electric boat makers soon began using the sun's energy to power their **motors**.

In 2009, Silent-Yachts began building its first solar-powered boat, the Solarwave 46.

Austrian boat company Silent-Yachts has specialized in **luxury** solar-powered boats since 2009.

Every Silent-Yachts boat has solar panels lining its roof. Everything from the **motor** to the lights to the refrigerator runs on solar power.

Silent-Yachts positions solar panels to get the greatest amount of energy from the sun.

Silent-Yachts's boats range in length from 59 to 120 feet (18 to 36.6 m). Their top speeds range from 18 to 23 miles per hour (29 to 37 kmh).

Silent-Yachts may not make the fastest electric boats. But its boats can get enough power from the sun to cross the ocean without stopping!

In 2018, the Silent 55 made its first appearance at the Cannes Yachting Festival.

CHAPTER 6

THE FUTURE'S ELECTRIC

Many boaters are concerned about gas-powered boats harming the **environment** with the gases they **release**. Electric boats allow people to travel on water without this effect.

Boat companies continue to improve electric boats to make them faster and more **affordable**. In the **future**, electric boats may rule the waves!

In 2012, the MS *Porrima* became the first solar EV to make it around the globe.

TIMELINE

1800s

Electric boats are invented.

1990s

Scientists **develop lithium-ion batteries** that can power **vehicles**.

1970

Duffy Electric Boats starts making modern electric boats.

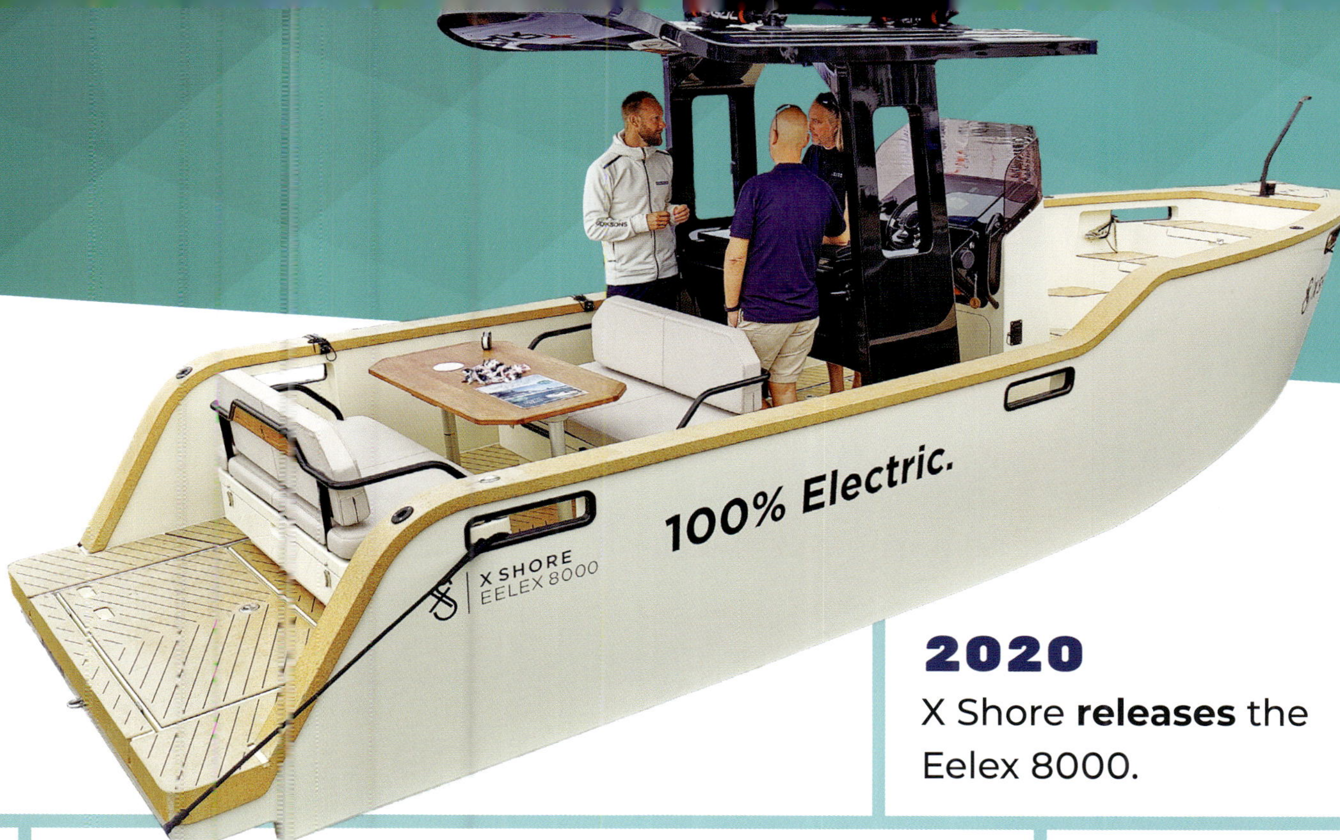

2009

Silent-Yachts starts creating solar-powered boats.

2020

X Shore **releases** the Eelex 8000.

2022

X Shore launches the X Shore 1.

GLOSSARY

affordable—having a cost that is not too high.

battery—a small container filled with chemicals that makes electrical power.

develop—to create something new over time.

environment—the natural world, including air, water, land, and animals.

expensive—having a high price.

future (FYOO-chuhr)—a time that has not yet occurred.

lithium-ion battery—a rechargeable battery that uses lithium ions as the primary component.

luxury—providing a high level of comfort and quality.

motor—a machine that produces motion or power for doing work.

recharge—to become charged again. Rechargeable means that something is able to be charged again.

release—to let go or make available to the public.

vehicle—something used for carrying persons or large objects. Some examples of vehicles are cars, trucks, boats, and airplanes.

volt—a unit for measuring the power of an electric current.

ONLINE RESOURCES

To learn more about electric boats, visit abdobooklinks.com. These links are routinely monitored and updated to provide the most current information available.

INDEX